JOHN LENNON
GREATEST HITS

Cover photo by Bob Gruen/Star File

ISBN 0-634-04654-3

HAL•LEONARD®
CORPORATION
7777 W. BLUEMOUND RD. P.O. BOX 13819 MILWAUKEE, WI 53213

Visit Hal Leonard Online at
www.halleonard.com

#9 Dream

Words and Music by John Lennon

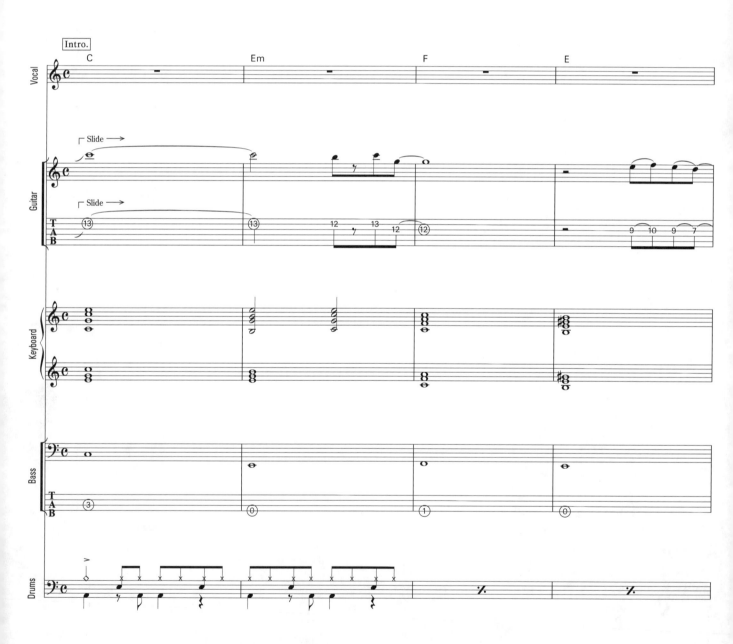

So _____ long a - go _____
know _____ yes, I know _____
Dream _____ dream a - way; _____
believe _____ yes, I believe; _____

3

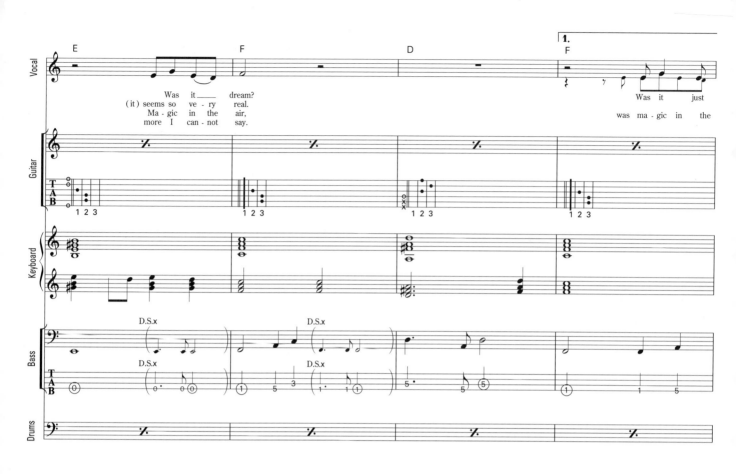

4

Took a   walk down ___ the
On a   riv - er ___ of

street
sound

through the heat   whis - pered
through the mir - ror ___ go

8

Cold Turkey

Words and Music by John Lennon and Paul McCartney

can't see no sky. ___
leave me a - lone. ___
free me a - gain. ___

My feet are so hea - vy
My eyes are wide o - pen
Oh I'll be a good___ boy

so is my head ___
can't get to sleep ___
please make me well ___

I wish I was a ba - by
one thing I'm sure___ of
I pro - mise you an - y - thing

I
I'm
get me

12

14

16

Happy Xmas (War Is Over)

Words and Music by John Lennon and Yoko Ono

Imagine

Words and Music by John Lennon

Instant Karma

Words and Music by John Lennon

Lyrics (Vocal):
In - stant Karma's ___ gon-na get you ___
In - stant Karma's ___ gon-na get you ___
In - stant Karma's ___ gon-na get you ___

What in the world you think -ing of

laugh -ing in the face of love,_____

what on earth __ you tryin' to do,___

it's up to you __

yeah___ you.___

34

Repeat & F.O.

Jealous Guy

Words and Music by John Lennon

I'm just a jea-lous guy.   2. I was feel-ing in-se-cure.___

You might not love me a-ny-more.___   I was shi-ver-ing___ in-side.

Love

Words and Music by John Lennon

Love is   real,_____

50

we can be;____   Love is   free,____

D.S.

Mind Games

Words and Music by John Lennon

59

Mother

Words and Music by John Lennon

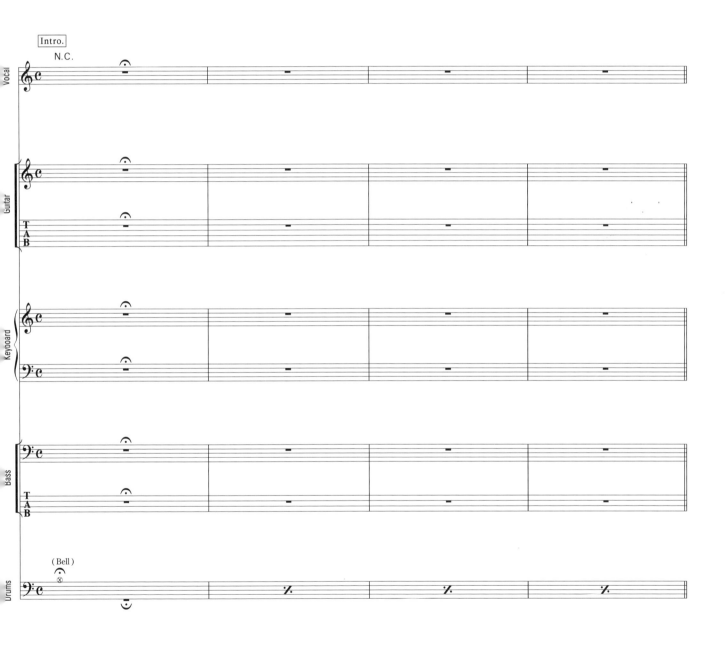

Nobody Told Me

Words and Music by John Lennon

No-bod-y told me there'd be days   like these.   No-bod-y told me there'd be days   like these.

Power to the People

Words and Music by John Lennon

Power to the people, power to the people,

power to the peo-ple. Power to the peo-ple right on.

Repeat & F.O.

Stand by Me

Words and Music by Ben E. King, Jerry Leiber and Mike Stoller

Repeat & F.O.

(Just Like) Starting Over

Words and Music by John Lennon

90

Repeat & F.O.

Whatever Gets You Through the Night

Words and Music by John Lennon

Hold me — darlin' — come on lis - ten to — me, I won't — do — you no

What-ev-er gets__ you to the

D.S.

Coda

Fade Out

Woman

Words and Music by John Lennon

Repeat & F.O.

NOTATION LEGEND

The music in this book is transcribed with the utmost attention to detail. However, it is recommended that you listen to the recording and pay close attention to subtle nuances and untranscribable rhythm of the music.

Please note that the music for each part is transcribed in a different format. For instance, for the male vocal, guitar and bass guitar parts, the music is noted an octave higher than the actual sounding pitch. The music for a keyboard instrument such as the piano is noted at actual pitch. Please keep the foregoing in mind when playing the keyboard part using a guitar.

Now we would like to explain the notation in this book for the guitar, the bass guitar and the drum parts respectively.

GUITAR

The following are the explanations for each symbol:

1) C : Bend
- C → Bend (whole step)
- HC → Bend (half step)
- 1HC → Bend (whole and half steps)
- 2C → Bend (two whole steps)
- QC → Slight Bend (microtone)

Letters or numbers printed before the C represent how high a note is to be bent.

2) U : Prebend (string bent before picking)
The U is considered different from C as the string is bent before picking.

3) D : Release
Release the bent string to its normal pitch. This D is equivalent to the latter half of Bend (or Prebend) and Release.

4) H : Hammer-On

5) P : Pull-Off

6) S : Legato Slide

7) tr : Trill (a combination of a fast Hammer-On/Pull-Off)

*Even if any of the above specified notes are combined with slurs, only the first note is to be struck.

8) gliss : Glissando
The Glissando is similar to the Legato Slide (S), however it does not designate exactly where the slide starts or where it ends. Since Glissando occur frequently, in some areas the note "gliss" may be omitted. Instead, slanted lines are used to express ascending and descending.

9) ~~~ : Vibrato

10) Harm : Natural Harmonic

11) (Ph): Pinch Harmonic
Add the edge of the thumb or the tip of the index finger of the pick hand to the normal pick attack.

12) ↓ : Tapping
Hammer the fret indicated with the pick hand finger.

13) ✕ : There are three meanings to this note.
1. A vague note which its actual pitch cannot be recognized.
2. A note impossible to tell its pitch (rare).
3. Fret-Hand muting with the left hand in a chord form (percussive tone).

BASS GUITAR

The notes are in bass clef (F clef). Some symbols for the bass are similar to those of the guitar, so it would be necessary for you to learn the above-mentioned guitar notations before you play.

DRUMS

From the space above the top line of the stave; G:Tom-tom, E:Snare drum, C:Bass tom-tom, A:Kick drum, ◇ on higher B:cymbal, ✕ on higher B:high hat (o → open, × → close), ✕ on lower F:high-hat (hit by pressing the pedal)